Federal Aid to Big Cities

James W. Fossett

Federal Aid to Big Cities:
The Politics of Dependence

THE BROOKINGS INSTITUTION
Washington, D.C.

Foreword

In the 1960s and 1970s, American cities became heavy users of grants-in-aid from the federal government. The amount of that aid increased under presidents of both parties, though with differences of approach among different administrations. The Democratic administrations of Lyndon B. Johnson and Jimmy Carter sought to concentrate federal aid on large cities with the highest levels of social and economic distress, while Republican presidents Richard M. Nixon and Gerald R. Ford, seeking to devolve power to local and state governments, advocated broad-gauged formula grants to a wide range of eligible governments. Today, almost all local governments in the country use federal grants-in-aid, but the biggest cities remain the primary users, judging by the relative size of their grants and by the share of their budgets supported by federal grants.

To assess how the increasing flow of federal grants was affecting local government and politics, the Governmental Studies Program of the Brookings Institution in 1978 undertook a series of case studies in large cities with financial support from the U.S. Department of Labor and Department of Commerce. Richard P. Nathan, then a senior fellow in the Governmental Studies Program, and James W. Fossett, then a research assistant in Governmental Studies, directed the project. Under their supervision, knowledgeable local observers—many of whom had been field associates in previous Brookings research on how federal programs worked on the local level—prepared individual reports. Ten reports were distributed, beginning in 1979, by the National Technical Information Service of the Commerce Department.

The Brookings Institution is pleased to publish Mr. Fossett's summary and interpretation of the case studies, *Federal Aid to Big*

Cities: The Politics of Dependence, and slightly condensed and updated versions of selected cases.

The central question that the project as a whole explores is to what extent large cities have become dependent on the federal government as a source of revenue. Synthesizing the findings from individual cities, Mr. Fossett argues that the answer depends on how a city uses that aid, which in turn depends on the city's fiscal condition, the amount of discretion it has in using federal funds, and the level of political organization among the beneficiaries of federal programs. Cities with major financial problems, considerable discretion in the use of federal dollars, and well-organized political systems are more likely than other cities to have become financially "dependent" on federal dollars, in the sense that they use substantial amounts of such funds to support basic city services. In those cities, elected officials are more actively involved in the allocation of federal funds than are officials in cities without these characterisitics.

Mr. Nathan, a ten-year veteran of Brookings' resident staff, is currently director of the Princeton Urban and Regional Research Center at the Woodrow Wilson School for Public and International Affairs, Princeton University, and a member of Brookings' associated staff. Mr. Fossett is a staff member at the Institute of Government and Public Affairs and the Department of Political Science at the University of Illinois.

The findings of Mr. Fossett and the case study authors are theirs alone and should not be ascribed to the Department of Labor, the Department of Commerce, or to the trustees, officers, or staff members of the Brookings Institution.

Bruce K. MacLaury
President

Washington, D.C.
March 1983

Contents

Tables

1. Introduction

Recent cuts in federal grant programs and Reagan administration proposals to delegate control over most urban programs to state governments seem likely to reopen debate about the extent to which state and local governments—particularly big-city governments—have become "dependent" on federal funds. A number of observers, noting the major build-up of federal grants to cities during the 1970s and the increasing size of these funds relative to local revenues, have argued that many city governments were in danger of becoming, in the words of one observer, "creatures of the state and wards of the federal government."

The changes during the 1970s were indeed substantial. The most important was a major increase in the amount of federal funds going to cities. This growth resulted from two initiatives: (1) the New Federalism proposals of the Nixon administration, which resulted in the adoption of general revenue sharing and the community development block grant (CDBG) and comprehensive employment and training (CETA) programs, and (2) the Carter administration's 1977 economic stimulus package, which substantially expanded funding for public service jobs, local public works, and countercyclical revenue sharing. Federal grants to cities grew by almost 700 percent over the 1970s, or almost twice the growth in nonwelfare grants and better than twice the growth rate in the grant system as a whole. Grants reached their peak as a city revenue source in 1978, when they provided funds equivalent to 26 percent of the revenue cities raised on their own and 70 percent of the revenue provided to cities by state governments. While the rate of growth in direct federal grants has declined sharply in recent years, federal dollars remain a substantial revenue source for city governments. In 1980, the most recent year for which data

1

are available, direct federal grants amounted to $10.9 billion, the equivalent of 23 percent of city-raised revenue.[1]

There were also noteworthy changes during the seventies in the geographic allocation of federal funds to cities. Under earlier categorical programs such as urban renewal and model cities, federal administrators reviewed applications from local agencies and granted funds to those that ranked high on various criteria. This method tended to concentrate federal funds in larger cities, particularly in the Northeast, whose officials were willing to invest substantial effort in developing applications and lobbying federal agencies to secure their approval.

The new programs of the seventies, by contrast, allocated funds automatically on the basis of formulas to all cities that met simple eligibility criteria. The general revenue sharing program, for example, distributes funds to all 38,000 units of general-purpose local government in the country. The community development block grant program provides nearly automatic funding to any city recognized as the central city of a Standard Metropolitan Statistical Area (SMSA). Governments do not have to compete for funds with other governments, but rather receive allocations based on characteristics of the city's population, housing stock, or finances. The increased use of formulas has had the effect of spreading funds to smaller cities and to larger cities located in the South and West, many of which had received little or no money from earlier programs.[2]

These new programs also produced a major change in the types of recipients within cities. Earlier categorical programs made large numbers of grants to special authorities and community organizations. The formula-based programs of the seventies, by contrast, provide federal funds to city governments, which have a substantial amount of discretion in deciding how to spend them. Organizations such as urban renewal authorities and community action agencies that once dealt directly with federal agencies are now compelled to work through city hall to obtain federal support.

1. U.S. Bureau of the Census, *City Government Finances in 1979–80* (Washington, D.C.: U.S. Government Printing Office, 1981), table 1.
2. For descriptions of changes in the geographic allocation of federal urban aid over this period, see Richard P. Nathan and James W. Fossett, "Urban Conditions—The Future of the Federal Role," in *1978 Proceedings of the Seventy-first Annual Conference on Taxation, Philadelphia* (Columbus, Ohio: National Tax Association—Tax Institute of America, 1979); and Richard P. Nathan, "The Outlook for Federal Grants to Cities," in Roy Bahl, ed., *The Fiscal Outlook for Cities* (Syracuse: Syracuse University Press, 1978).

There is, in brief, some plausibility to the argument that cities may have become "dependent" on federal dollars. More money is being provided to more cities than earlier, and being provided in a form that makes it relatively easy for city officials either to cut local taxes or to increase services with no increase in taxes. Further, redirecting federal funds through city hall may have provided mayors and council members with the opportunity to use federal funds to maintain or broaden their base of political support. If local officials have availed themselves of these opportunities for fiscal or political relief, then many cities may have in fact become "dependent" on these funds and stand to lose substantially from aid cutbacks of the magnitude contained in recent administration proposals.

The extent to which cities have, in fact, used federal dollars in ways that have made them financially or politically "dependent" on these funds is, however, far from clear. Because the federal programs enacted during the seventies presented local officials with a considerable amount of discretion in how to use federal dollars, a reasonable assessment of "dependence" requires some understanding of the uses of federal dollars and the attitudes of state and local officials toward them.

This essay presents such an assessment, drawing on case studies of the impact of federal funds on eleven large American cities in 1978. It first indicates the difficulties associated with current definitions of city "dependence" on federal funds, and then advances an alternative definition of dependence based on city use of federal funds to support "basic" city services. It presents a set of propositions about the political and financial conditions under which cities become "dependent" on federal funds and suggests the likely consequences of recent budget cutbacks on the finances and politics of big cities.

Measuring Dependence—Current Practices

Most attempts to assess the impact of grants on city budgets simply compare the amount of federal aid a city receives with other types of city income, usually taxes or total revenues from the city's own sources. The logic behind this approach is simple: Cities that receive large amounts of federal money relative to other local income are more vulnerable to budget disruptions caused by reductions in federal money—hence more dependent on that money—than are cities for which federal funds are a less significant revenue source. A number of scholars and government agencies have relied on such calculations to assess the "dependence" of different cities at different points over the last several years.[3]

Most researchers who have made these calculations have predicted dire consequences from a major reduction in federal grants to cities. Most large cities, according to these calculations, receive large amounts of federal money relative to the revenue that they raise on their own and have come to rely, both financially and politically, on these funds either to keep taxes down or to support city services at levels that could not be sustained in the absence of federal funds. Substantial cuts in federal funds would require either massive cuts in city services or equally sizeable increases in city taxes and produce significant deterioration in the financial condition and credit position of most big cities. In short, American cities are "dependent" on federal funds and have been for some time.[4]

The major argument of this essay is that this sort of "dependence" calculation overstates the financial and political importance of federal funds to most cities and hence the potential consequences of a major reduction in that aid. Although some cities have come to rely quite heavily on federal funds—in brief, are "dependent" on them—there are fewer such cities than is commonly believed.

Redefining Dependence

As noted, the major measure of "dependence" currently in the literature on federal grants is the amount of federal money a city receives relative to various sorts of locally generated revenue. Figures of this sort can be useful indicators of trends in the distribution of federal funds and the relative size of federal dollars in local budgets. They need to be carefully interpreted, however, because several factors can produce substantial variations in either local or federal revenues, but have little connection to city "de-

3. See, for example, the calculations reported in U.S. Department of the Treasury, "Report on the Impact of the Economic Stimulus Package on 48 Large Urban Governments" (Washington, D.C.: Department of the Treasury, unpublished, 1978); Advisory Commission on Intergovernmental Relations, *Federal Stabilization Policy: The Role of State and Local Governments* (Washington, D.C.: U.S. Government Printing Office, 1978); and Astrid Mergit, "Fiscal Dependency of American Cities," *Public Budgeting and Finance*, vol. 1, no. 2 (1981).

4. For pessimistic assessments drawing on these results, see Roy Bahl, Bernard Jump, Jr., and Larry Schroeder, "The Outlook for City Fiscal Performance in Declining Regions," in Bahl, *Fiscal Outlook* and John Petersen, "Big City Borrowing Costs and Credit Quality," in Robert Burchell and David Listokin, eds., *Cities Under Stress* (New Brunswick, N.J.: Rutgers University Press, 1981), among others.

pendence" on federal funds. The following five factors are particularly important.

1. *Support from the state or other overlying governments.* Some cities receive large amounts of relatively unrestricted funds from other governments to finance activities that other cities are required to fund with local tax revenue. According to Census Bureau figures, Rochester, N.Y., received $110 million in 1980 from the state of New York and other local governments (largely from Monroe County), more than twice the amount it received from the federal government and only $15 million less than what it raised on its own. By contrast, Tulsa received only $4.3 million either from Oklahoma or from other local governments—about 3 percent of its own-source revenue and less than 15 percent of what it received from the federal government. Federal aid is a much larger percentage of local revenue in Rochester than in Tulsa, but this difference may be partly due to the fact that Tulsa finances almost all its budget from its own resources, while Rochester receives substantial funds from other outside sources.

2. *Functions for which a city is responsible.* Metropolitan areas vary widely in the way various functions are divided among different local governments. New York City, for example, is responsible for partial financing of both the aid to families with dependent children (AFDC) and medicaid programs; operates a school system, a city university system, a public housing system, a sewer system, and a park system; and subsidizes both the city transit and hospital systems. In Chicago, by contrast, all of these functions are performed by special districts or by other levels of government for which the city has no direct financial responsibility.[5] These differences affect both the range of activities that cities support with tax revenue and the amount of federal support they receive, since public housing, education, transit, and sewer systems all receive substantial federal support, but are not connected in any simple way to the importance of federal money in city budgets.

3. *The level of service the city provides.* A city whose citizens want a relatively limited level of services will tax less, and hence appear to be more "dependent," than a city receiving the same amount of federal money whose citizens prefer a higher level of city services and are willing to pay for it through higher taxes. As a

5. For a detailed description of the way these differences in responsibility affect local spending patterns, see Richard P. Nathan and Paul R. Dommel, "The Cities," in Joseph Pechman, ed., *Setting National Priorities: The 1978 Budget* (Washington, D.C.: Brookings Institution, 1977).

crude example, New York City supported approximately 150 workers per 10,000 residents in 1978 to provide such basic services as police, fire, and sanitation, while Houston employed only 63 workers for every 10,000 residents to provide the same services. Other things being equal, New York might be expected to have a higher tax level than Houston in order to support this higher level of service. This difference in service levels, however, is not affected in any simple way by the amount of federal money either city receives.

4. *The price of providing a given level of service.* Differences among cities in prevailing local wages and the costs of equipment, materials, and transportation require some cities to pay more tax money than others to support the same level of service. Environmental Protection Agency figures indicate, for example, that the same sewer would cost 50 percent more to construct in New York than it costs in Houston. Such differences in price levels, like differences in services, affect local taxes, but have no necessary relationship to how important federal money is to the city's budget.

5. *The proportion of federal funds a city uses to support its own agencies.* Many cities allocated part of their CETA grants to other local governments or to community-based organizations, and some cities delegated significant portions of CDBG funds to community groups. Funds treated in this way show up in a city's budget as revenue from the federal government, but because they support no direct city activities it is difficult to argue that their presence constitutes city "dependence" on federal money.

These differences among cities in the organization and financing of local government indicate that differences in "dependence," as currently defined and calculated, may reflect differences in the functions for which cities are responsible or the level of assistance they receive from state governments rather than differences in the importance of grant dollars in local budgets. Current measures of "dependence," in short, may produce misleading results about the relative importance of grant dollars on the budgets of different American cities.

Perhaps more importantly, calculations of this sort do little to reveal the importance of federal funds to city finances because they do not indicate the types of services that cities use federal dollars to support. It is impossible to tell what a city uses federal money for from the overall amount of money it receives, yet knowing how aid is spent is crucial to judging the degree of a city's dependence.

More precisely, cities that rely heavily on federal funds to supply "basic" or "core" services can be judged to be more "dependent" on those funds than those that use the funds for other purposes. Regardless of what else they do, almost all cities provide police and fire protection, pick up garbage, build and maintain city streets and other public infrastructure, and maintain an administrative structure. Even in the most conservative cities, these activities are seen as legitimate functions of city government, enjoy a relatively broad base of support, and are considered to be legitimate claimants on the city budget that should be supported at adequate levels before other services are provided.

By contrast, cities vary widely in the extent to which they provide such services as manpower training or other social services, health services, housing assistance, and cultural activities. These activities are less universally accepted as legitimate city functions, and their base of political support and claim on city resources are less well established than those of the "basic" services. Hence they are more likely to be dependent on outside resources and more likely to be cut in the event of budget difficulties.

The basic services historically have been financed with locally raised revenue at levels determined by local officials, and have generally been the last services to be cut in the event of financial problems. Use of federal funds to support these services carries the implication that local revenues are not sufficient to maintain these services at minimal levels and that no alternative sources of support exist, since other services have already been reduced.

This formulation suggests that such factors as the condition of the city budget, the attitudes of local decision makers and interest groups, and the amount of discretion provided in the use of grants are likely to be the most important determinants of what cities do with federal funds and how "dependent" they are on these dollars. The next section of this essay addresses these questions.

2. Budgetary and Political Context

Most existing models of the allocation of federal grants by state and local governments assume that the use of federal funds is driven by the same forces that influence the allocation of other local revenue. More precisely, most models make two general assumptions about the character of federal money and the political forces that affect its allocation:

1. that local officials view federal dollars in much the same way as local funds, in that there is no risk or uncertainty, either actual or perceived, associated with their continuation; and

2. that federal funds are allocated through the same political channels, by the same actors, and in response to the same set of political constraints as other sources of revenue.[1]

This essay assumes, to the contrary, that unless they have pressing reasons to do so, elected officials (1) will not pump large

---

1. Most such models rely either on extensions of consumer choice theory in which the median local voter is the effective decision maker or on simulations of the allocation of resources among various functions that local governments perform. While clear statements of these assumptions are rare, neither set of models explicitly incorporates the possibility of either actual or perceived uncertainty associated with federal funds and both explain the allocation of federal funds in terms of the same factors that influence the use of local funds—the preferences of the median voter in one case and standing decision rules about the division of additional funds between local functions in the other. See, for example, Paul Courant, Edward Gramlich and Daniel Rubinfeld, "The Stimulative Effects of Intergovernmental Grants: Or Why Money Sticks Where It Hits" in Peter Mieszkowski and William Oakland, eds., *Fiscal Federalism and Grants-in-Aid* (Urban Institute, 1979) and Patrick D. Larkey, *Evaluating Public Programs: The Impact of General Revenue Sharing on Municipal Government* (Princeton University Press, 1979). Larkey recognizes the possibility of risk averse behavior and allocation of federal funds outside the normal budget process, but gives no indication of how his results would be modified in either of these cases.

amounts of federal money into local operating budgets, because of uncertainty related to federal aid, and (2) will not become closely involved in allocating federal funds among competing uses and beneficiaries, because of the political risks involved in doing so.

Uncertain Funding Levels

The most important reason for uncertainty is the possibility of cuts in funding levels. With the exception of general revenue sharing, all major federal urban aid programs are subject to the annual appropriations process and all have relatively short authorization periods (in most cases three years or less). Some education programs are "forward funded"—that is, funds are appropriated a year before they are spent—but for most federal programs both the amount of money available and the terms under which these funds are available are subject to frequent and unpredictable changes.

These changes can have substantial impact on city budgets. When Congress let the economic stimulus package expire in 1978, for example, some cities lost aid amounting to more than 10 percent of local tax revenues. At the same time, Congress imposed new restrictions on the eligibility, wages, and tenure of participants in the PSE program that made it much harder to use these funds to support regular city services. Local governments that had used these funds to support normal city activities were required to either reduce services to match cuts, increase local taxes to continue services, or invest time and effort lobbying the Department of Labor for waivers of the new PSE requirements.[2]

Regulatory Requirements

A second source of uncertainty for local officials is enforcement of rules governing uses and beneficiaries of federal funds. Grant programs adopted during the seventies reduced federal influence over local decisions, but federal agencies still interpret and enforce regulations on such matters as participant and project eligibility as well as affirmative action and environmental impact requirements. Federal agency "signals" to local governments about what is and is not permissible under particular programs and

2. For a description of these changes, see Richard P. Nathan and James W. Fossett, "Statement on Urban Policy" (testimony before the Revenue Sharing Subcommittee of the Senate Finance Committee, March 12, 1979); and William Mirengoff *et al., The New CETA: Effects on Public Service Employment Programs* (Washington, D.C.: Department of Labor, 1980).

the strength with which these signals are enforced are important variables in determining local use of funds.

These "signals" are, however, also subject to change. Congressional complaints, adverse media coverage, and changes in federal agency personnel can cause sudden shifts. The community development block grant program is a case in point. Under the Ford administration, the Department of Housing and Urban Development (HUD) allowed local governments considerable freedom to decide what types of programs would be funded and which areas of cities would be eligible to benefit. When the Carter administration began, new officials at HUD adopted regulations requiring local governments to spend the bulk of CDBG funds on activities that would primarily benefit low- and moderate-income groups. This change in agency "signals" forced some local governments to alter geographic spending patterns substantially and change the types of activities they supported with CDBG funds.[3] More recently, the Reagan administration has abolished many of the Carter regulations, once again allowing local governments to spend CDBG money as they please.

Uncertainty about the level and form of federal aid makes local officials hesitant to use substantial amounts of federal money in the city's operating budget. In the event of funding cutbacks or significant rule changes, officials would be forced to choose between raising local taxes or reducing services, thus alienating either local taxpayers or recipients of federally funded services. Officials naturally want to avoid such a situation.

Political Control and Utilization

Gaining political control over federally funded programs is also potentially risky for local elected officials. Federal funds do provide jobs and contracts that can be used as a political resource to reward supporters as well as to provide services at no cost to local taxpayers. Nevertheless, mayors and council members have reason to avoid taking an active role in the management of federally supported programs.

Three considerations help account for this reluctance. First, the uncertainty of federal funding may make it unwise to use federal funds as a means of generating or maintaining political support

3. See Paul R. Dommel *et al., Targeting Community Development* (Washington, D.C.: U.S. Department of Housing and Urban Development, 1980), chapters 1 and 6.

through patronage or award of contracts. Funding cutbacks or changes in regulations may leave officials with more claimants than they can satisfy with local funds. As a result, local officials may find it expedient to avoid creating expectations that they may not be able to fulfill in the future.

Second, involvement with some federally funded programs may attract opposition from politically important groups. Some groups view public service employment as "make work" or "leaf raking," or object to the subsidized housing requirements attached to the community development block grant program. In many cities, the risk of generating such opposition may be greater than the potential benefits that a local official would gain by becoming involved in these programs. While the community development and CETA programs have increased the incentive for representatives of minorities and disadvantaged groups to participate in electoral politics by channeling grants to city hall rather than to community groups, many such groups may still lack the ability to deliver votes or other support to elected officials in exchange for program funding. In cities where party systems are relatively weak, where political participation has been historically low, or where most officials are elected at large, representatives of minority groups may have found it inordinately difficult to develop a base of support that would enable them to bargain effectively with local elected officials. In such cases, local officials have little incentive to devote much attention to the operations of federally funded programs, since the return in electoral or other support is likely to be small.

Finally, regulations governing the use of federal funds may not provide enough discretion to provide political benefits for mayors or councils in allocation decisions. All cities are subject to the same regulations, but those regulations have different effects in different cities. For example, the Carter administration's regulations requiring cities to concentrate CDBG spending in low- and moderate-income areas define "low and moderate income" by reference to the median income of the entire metropolitan area. As a result, cities with high median incomes relative to their suburbs are more restricted in where they can spend CDBG funds than are the poor cities. In Phoenix, for example, only one-fifth of the census tracts had median family incomes that qualified as "low and moderate" relative to the metropolitan area median income, while in Boston more than 60 percent of the tracts were eligible. In a city like Phoenix, relatively few officials have an opportunity to benefit politically from the allocation of federal funds and few neighbor-hood groups are interested in how and where these funds are spent. As a result, there is little incentive for local officials to become actively involved in the allocation of these dollars.

Minimizing Political Risks

In short, the level and form of federal funds cannot be accu-rately forecast from one year to the next, and the political costs associated with public involvement with federal funds may be substantial and the benefits minimal. It is reasonable, therefore, to expect local officials to be cautious about relying on these dollars either as support for ongoing city activities or as a source of political capital.

Local officials are likely to use any or all of several approaches that minimize political risks involved in use of federal funds. They may allocate those funds outside the normal budget process or spend them primarily for capital projects or nonrecurring operat-ing expenses that could be discontinued with little trouble. Elected officials may also put some political distance between themselves and federal programs by allowing program staffs to make most major decisions about where to spend federal aid. Del-egating these decisions allows elected officials to avoid being identified with federally funded activities by groups opposed to them and makes them less vulnerable to demands to continue fed-erally supported programs if these funds were to be terminated.

Description of Case Studies

In order to investigate the impact of federal funds on local finances and politics in a fashion that provides evidence on what cities have used federal dollars to support and the ways in which these dollars have affected local politics, field associates of the Brookings Institution conducted a series of case studies on the impact of federal grants in eleven large cities as of 1978. The stud-ies were made under contract between Brookings and the U.S. Departments of Labor and Commerce. The cities selected for examination, described in table 1, vary widely in rates of popula-tion and economic growth, financial condition, political structure and culture, experience with earlier federal programs, and most other characteristics that might be expected to affect their use of federal funds. The authors of the studies are locally based econo-mists and political scientists selected by a central staff at Brook-ings for their knowledge of city finances and politics. All had participated in earlier field network evaluation studies of the general revenue sharing, public service employment, and community development block grant programs.[4] The case studies were prepared according to a common analytical framework developed jointly by the central staff and the field associates, which consists of four basic sets of questions:

1. *To what extent have cities become dependent on federal funds to pay for basic services?* As argued earlier, the total amount of federal aid a city receives provides little indication of the services it uses federal dollars to support or of the city's ability to continue financing these services if funds were discontinued. Use of federal funds to support basic city services is a better indicator of city "dependence" on federal money than the total amount of such funds the city receives.

These case studies use a variety of approaches to determine the extent to which a city is dependent on federal funds. Each case study reports not only on the share of the city budget supported by federal dollars, but also on the services supported by those dollars and local ability and willingness to continue the activities supported by federal money if these funds were discontinued. Because it deals not only with how much money a city gets but also with what the city would do if aid were curtailed, this approach provides a broader view than other studies of the political and financial importance of federal grants to cities.

2. *What was the impact of the Carter Administration's economic stimulus package (ESP) on local finances and unemployment levels?* All three programs in the ESP were designed to increase employment and enhance local recovery from the recession of 1973–75, but through very different approaches. The antirecession fiscal assistance (ARFA) program provided funds to local governments in areas of high unemployment to pay employee salaries, with the intent of preventing governments from responding to revenue losses by laying off personnel. The local public works (LPW) program attempted to stimulate employment in the construction industry by providing grants for construction and rehabilitation of public facilities. The public service employment (PSE) program provided public jobs to long-term unemployed persons through grants to state and local governments, which could hire

---

4. For a description of these studies, see Richard P. Nathan, "The Methodology for Field Network Evaluation Studies," in Walter Williams, ed., *Studying Implementation* (Chatham, N.J.: Chatham House, 1981).

Table 1. *Population, Urban Hardship, and Economic Growth in Case Study Cities*

City	1977 Population	Urban conditions index, 1975[a]	Percentage change in			
			Value added, manufacturing, 1972–76	Retail sales, 1972–77	Wholesale sales, 1972–77	Selected service receipts, 1972–77
New York	7,257,787	222	3.9	14.7	64.1	8.2
Chicago	3,062,881	255	22.8	19.5	33.2	18.7
Los Angeles	2,761,222	89	49.3	49.3	76.3	59.2
Houston	1,554,960	40	85.5	85.5	NA	158.1
Detroit	1,289,910	266	24.8	9.0	12.5	–17.3
Phoenix	864,516	21	50.5	56.9	69.8	58.2
Boston	618,493	303	15.8	12.5	19.3	37.5
Cleveland	609,187	400	28.8	17.4	16.8	14.6
St. Louis	517,671	487	37.8	17.5	73.0	12.8
Tulsa	334,365	57	62.4	62.4	NA	62.6
Rochester	256,285	266	32.5	5.7	–7.7	34.6

Sources: Population: Bureau of Census, *City Government Finances in 1977–78;* Urban conditions index: Paul R. Dommel, *Decentralizing Community Development* (Washington, D.C.: U.S. Government Printing Office, 1979), appendix II; 1972–1976/77 figures: James W. Fossett and Richard P. Nathan, "The Prospects for Urban Revival," in Roy Bahl, ed., *Urban Government Finances: Emerging Trends* (Beverly Hills, Calif.: Sage Publications, 1981).

a. The urban conditions index is a three-factor index that combines population and concentration of older housing and poverty. The mean of this index is standardized at 100. Cities with index scores above 100 are more distressed than the average; those with scores below 100 are less distressed.

individuals on their own payrolls or subcontract hiring to community organizations or other governments.

All three of these programs had been enacted under the Ford administration, but were roughly doubled in size when reenacted or extended in 1977. As noted earlier, the Carter administration's attempts to convert the ESP programs into permanent, structurally oriented programs when the stimulus package expired in 1978 were unsuccessful. These case studies assess the effectiveness of the ESP programs in promoting local economic and budgetary recovery, describe the advantages and disadvantages of each program as it was operated locally, and indicate some of the results of the programs' termination or reduction.

3. *Who benefits from federally supported programs?* Federal programs vary widely in the extent to which they regulate the types of services local governments can provide with federal funds and the income groups or areas which can receive these services. Some federal programs, such as the school lunch program operated by the Department of Agriculture, require local governments to spend federal money on specified services for particular income groups or areas; others specify who must be served, but allow local governments to decide how to serve them; still other programs define the service to be provided, but impose no restrictions on beneficiaries. These case studies report on which income groups in each city are the major direct beneficiaries of the programs supported by federal funds, using a common method for classifying benefits to different groups in the population. The studies identify the major political and programmatic factors that influence the distribution of benefits.

4. *Who decides how federal money will be spent?* As noted earlier, grant programs adopted in the seventies were designed to take power over decisions on the use of federal funds away from appointed officials and give it to elected officials such as mayors and legislators. This redistribution of power was to be achieved by making grants to city governments rather than to special authorities or nongovernmental organizations and by requiring both the mayor and the city council to approve proposed uses of funds.

While these procedural changes provide elected officials with considerable potential influence over how federal funds are allocated, they do not ensure that mayors and councils will, in fact, exercise that potential. Officials in some cities may choose, for reasons suggested earlier, not to involve themselves actively in these decisions, allowing professional staffs and concerned interest groups to determine how federal funds are to be allocated. These case studies describe the political process by which federal money is allocated in each city, identify the actors and groups that have played major roles in this process, and assess how federal grants have affected local decision making and politics.

The next sections of this essay report on the amount of federal funds the cities described in these case studies received and spent in 1978, their "dependence" on these funds measured in various ways, the income groups that benefited from federally supported programs, and the financial and political factors that have influenced their use of federal dollars. More precisely, it will be argued that city "dependence" on federal funds to support basic city services is largely determined by local financial conditions. Cities with recurring financial problems have a strong incentive to use federal dollars to finance local services, while more prosperous places have equally strong incentives to use grant dollars to pay for services that enjoy less political support and create fewer continuing claims on local budgets. By contrast, the income incidence of programs supported by federal funds is influenced more strongly by the politics surrounding the allocation of grant dollars. In cities that have a considerable amount of discretion in using federal funds and where the constituents of federal programs are relatively well organized, decisions about the use of federal funds are more likely to be made by elected officials and the benefits from these dollars to be dispersed relatively widely among income groups. On the other hand, in cities that have less discretion and less constituent organization, decisions about how to spend federal dollars are more likely to be made by professional program staff and the benefits from these dollars to be more concentrated among lower income groups.

Remeasuring Dependence

Table 2 shows the total amount of funds that the eleven cities received and spent in 1978, divided between operating and capital purposes. Table 3 displays different measures of "dependence" on federal funds spent for operating purposes. Column 1 of table 3 displays the size of federal operating funds as a percentage of local tax revenue, which has been frequently reported as a measure of "dependence." These figures suggest conditions not dissimilar from those reported by other observers—extensive reliance on federal funds as a source of operating support. On average, the amount of federal aid these cities used for operating purposes in 1978 was equal to 43.3 percent of city tax revenues. In eight cities, federal funds were equivalent to over 40 percent of local tax revenues, and in three—Phoenix, Cleveland, and Detroit—this figure was in excess of 50 percent. Based on these figures, most, if not all, of these cities would have to be judged as "dependent" on federal funds.

The next two columns of table 3 show the fraction of federal operating funds spent on "basic services" and the amount of local expenditures on basic services accounted for by federal dollars.[5] These figures suggest both a lower level of "dependence" on federal funds overall and a very different distribution of reliance on federal funds than suggested by the figures in the first column. Although total federal aid for operating purposes amounts to a large share of city finances if measured against local taxes, less than 40 percent of the money was used to fund departments that provide "basic" services. This portion of the aid amounted to, on average, less than 20 percent of city expenditures for these services. Neither of these fractions is negligible, but they do suggest that city "dependence" on federal money, at least over this period, was considerably lower than prevailing wisdom might suggest.

Perhaps more importantly, these figures suggest that the amount of federal money a city receives relative to its own taxes has little relationship to the city's propensity to spend those funds on basic services. Of the six cities with above-average ratios of aid to tax revenues, only three—Cleveland, Detroit, and St. Louis—spent greater than average shares of these funds on basic services. The other three cities—Rochester, Boston, and New York—spent substantial amounts of federal money to support basic services but received smaller than average amounts of aid relative to local taxes. By contrast, several cities, such as Phoenix and Chicago, received large amounts of federal funds relative to their own taxes but spent smaller than average fractions of these funds for basic services. Put simply, next to nothing can be inferred about what a city does with federal money from how much federal money it gets.

The next sections of this essay discuss the factors that may have produced differences in the process of allocating federal funds and indicate how these differences produced different patterns of spending.

5. As used here, "basic services" includes those activities corresponding to the Census Bureau's expenditure categories of public safety, public works, sanitation, and general administration. Education has also been included as a basic service for New York and Boston, since both cities operate the local school system as a city department, and its political claim on the city budget in these cities is as strong as that of other departments that provide services more commonly labeled as "basic."

Table 2. *Federal Aid by Type, Fiscal Year 1978*
(thousands of dollars)

City	Carryover obligations and allocations from FY 1977	Federal obligations and allocations, FY 1978	Total federal aid available, FY 1978	Federal aid funds expenditures, FY 1978	Carryover obligations and allocations to FY 1979
Detroit					
Operating	68,948	122,504	191,252	176,225	14,911
Capital	114,893	72,146	187,039	75,817	110,166
Total	183,841	194,650	382,291	252,042	125,077
Phoenix					
Operating	3,934	61,960	65,894	66,200	(306)
Capital	NA	27,230	27,230	23,978	3,252
Total	3,934	89,190	93,124	90,178	2,946
Los Angeles					
Operating	NA	NA	347,589	274,898	72,691
Capital	NA	NA	198,045	38,036	160,009
Total	NA	NA	545,634	312,934	232,700
Tulsa					
Operating	3,408	18,862	22,310	20,682	1,588
Capital	4,877	6,965	11,843	4,560	7,283
Total	8,285	25,826	34,153	25,242	8,970
Rochester					
Operating	422	26,293	26,716	23,529	NA
Capital	15,952	19,923	35,875	17,297	NA
Total	16,375	46,216	62,590	40,826	NA

Chicago					
Operating	86,674	522,766	609,440	332,238	277,202
Capital	136,399	155,782	292,181	91,762	200,419
Total	223,073	678,548	901,621	424,000	477,621
Boston					
Operating	NA	NA	NA	156,778	NA
Capital	NA	NA	NA	38,497	NA
Total	NA	NA	NA	195,275	NA
St. Louis					
Operating	24,440	74,646	99,086	67,754	31,332
Capital	18,235	43,373	61,608	15,452	46,156
Total	42,675	118,019	160,694	83,206	77,488
Cleveland					
Operating	NA	NA	NA	67,541	NA
Capital	NA	NA	NA	14,028	NA
Total	NA	NA	NA	81,569	NA
Houston					
Operating	49,437	70,262	119,699	84,681	35,018
Capital	119,939	140,356	332,296	126,101	206,194
Total	241,377	210,618	451,995	210,782	241,213
New York City[a]					
Operating	NA	NA	1,219,700	1,199,700	20,000
Capital	NA	NA	2,079,400	423,900	1,655,500
Total	NA	NA	3,299,100	1,623,600	1,675,500

Source: Federal aid case studies.

a. Excludes AFDC, medicaid, and title XX.

Table 3. *Three Measures of Dependence on Federal Funds, 1978*

City	*Federal operating grants as percentage of local taxes*	*Percentage of federal operating grants spent on basic services*	*Federal operating grants for basic services as percentage of total spending on basic services*
Phoenix	66.0	30.2	14.7
Cleveland	58.4	46.0	24.0
Detroit	52.4	49.0[a]	25.5
Chicago	49.6	28.7	10.9
St. Louis	44.0	49.9[a]	27.0
Los Angeles	41.6	10.3	4.5
Tulsa	40.1	18.3	11.3
Rochester	36.8	92.4	22.3
Boston	36.4	39.3	13.0
Houston	31.0	16.5	4.4
New York[b]	19.5	55.3	22.7
Average, eleven cities	43.3	39.6	16.4

Source: Case study reports.

Note: Basic services include public safety, public works, sanitation, and general administration. For New York and Boston, schools have also been added.

a. Estimated on the basis of employment.

b. Excludes AFDC and medicaid from federal funds received.

3. Explaining Grant Politics

As argued earlier, city officials have considerable incentives to avoid relying on federal funds as a source of support for ongoing city programs or as political resources, largely because of uncertainty about whether the aid will continue. The inability to predict how much federal revenue will be available from year to year and the restrictions on its use create a strong incentive for local officials to spend federal money for activities that could be discontinued without establishing a permanent claim on the city budget or to allocate it outside the normal budget process altogether by leaving decisions about its use to program staff.

In some cities, however, these incentives may have been ineffective. In these cities, mayors and councils have been actively involved in allocating federal funds, substantial amounts of which have been used to support basic city services. Three factors appear to distinguish those cities where federal dollars have become politically and financially important from those where these funds have largely been allocated by staff outside the normal budget process. These factors are (1) the city's financial condition, (2) the degree of discretion the city has in deciding how to allocate federal money, and (3) the level of political organization in the city, combined with attitudes of city officials toward federal money. The following sections discuss each factor, showing why it is important and how the cities can be grouped according to each of these factors.

Financial Condition

The most important of these factors has been the city's financial condition. Cities with relatively few financial problems are likely to use federal aid cautiously. These cities can adequately support normal city services from their own resources, so they can afford to insulate themselves from the uncertainty surrounding federal funds by using these dollars for activities that create no permanent claim on the city budget. One might expect that such cities would use large amounts of federal dollars to support such activities as social services or expansion of maintenance and clean-up activities of various sorts. Some such cities may delegate federally funded activities to other governments or community groups as much as possible. Because officials in these cities wish to avoid any political claim on city funds if federal programs are discontinued, they are likely to allocate little city money to the activities supported by federal dollars.

In cities with more severe financial problems, officials might be expected to adopt a different attitude toward the appropriate uses of federal money. If local revenues are not sufficient to cover desired levels of expenditures on such services as police, fire, and streets, then local officials are unlikely to be able to afford caution. Using federal funds to expand social services or other "secondary" activities while laying off police officers or firefighters would make local officials vulnerable to attack both from organized municipal employees and from voters who support the continuation of basic services but are less enthusiastic about expanding social services. Because the beneficiaries of social services may be less well organized and thus less able to obtain separate treatment for the funds that provide these services, local officials in hard-pressed cities may find it expedient to use federal funds as a source of support for ongoing basic city activities.

The uncertainty of federal aid is less likely to concern officials in cities with a high degree of fiscal pressure, because they already are likely to be living from budget to budget. For these officials, the immediate problem of balancing the current year's accounts is likely to take precedence over the future problem of possible cuts in federal funds. Moreover, if federal funds are withdrawn, these officials can convincingly plead poverty and eliminate the federally supported program with less political risk than officials in more prosperous cities. Because federal dollars are probably the most significant source of uncommitted revenue available in hard-pressed cities, officials in these cities have reason to use these dollars to maintain ongoing city services and even to lobby federal officials to relax regulations against using grant money for these purposes.

Persistent shortages of city revenue also affect the politics surrounding the budget process. As students of organization theory have frequently argued, decisions on how to allocate resources are made at a higher level in the organizational hierarchy when resources are scarce than when there is plenty of "slack." Because there are fewer resources to satisfy competing demands from various groups in the organization, higher levels of authority must be invoked to decide how resources will be divided than would be the case if the amount of slack were greater.[1] This argument suggests that mayors and city budget officials in hard-pressed cities will spend more time trying to control expenditures and to locate additional sources of revenue than officials in more prosperous places. For example, decisions on whether or not to fill vacant positions would be made by department heads in more prosperous places but in hard-pressed cities are more likely to be made by central budget staff or through mayorally imposed guidelines.

Fiscal pressure also creates a strong incentive for mayors and budget officials to "create slack" by centralizing control over the allocation of discretionary revenue, including federal funds. Over the period under consideration here, for example, the law imposed virtually no limits on the number of laid-off city employees that a city could hire with public service employment funds, the length of time a PSE worker could stay in the program, or the salary that could be paid participants. In this situation, cities could relatively easily convert PSE funds into a source of support for ongoing city activities. Therefore, one might expect that mayors and budget officials of hard-pressed cities would be more involved in the allocation of these funds than their counterparts in more prosperous places, and that hard-pressed cities would be more likely to use PSE funds to support normal city services.[2]

1. See, for example, Michael Cohen, James March, and Johan P. Olson, "A Garbage Can Model of Organizational Choice," *Administrative Science Quarterly*, vol. 17 (March 1972).

2. See Janet Galchick, "Local Variations in Implementing Public Service Employment: An Analysis of Process and Outcomes" (Princeton, N.J.: Princeton Urban and Regional Research Center, unpublished, 1981) for a more detailed statement of this argument.

Classifying Cities by Financial Condition

Although classifying a city's financial condition is difficult to do precisely, the cities under consideration here can be divided with some confidence into two groups of roughly equal size. Over the middle seventies, New York, Cleveland, Detroit, St. Louis, Rochester, and Boston operated under relatively stringent financial conditions, while Chicago, Los Angeles, Houston, Tulsa, and Phoenix were under relatively less pressure. This division is based on the relative rates of growth in revenues and expenditures and on the relative conditions of general funds.

As the figures in table 1 suggest, economic growth over the middle seventies in the cities classified as hard pressed was substantially slower than in the more prosperous places. Value added by manufacturing grew by an average of 24 percent in the hard-pressed cities, compared with 54 percent in the cities classified as more prosperous. Differences in growth rates in retail sales and service receipts were equally substantial. As a result of these disparities, the more prosperous cities realized substantial growth in local revenues and city employment, while the budgets of harder-pressed cities grew at a slower rate in spite of increases in local tax rates, in some cases major ones. On average, general fund revenues grew at an annual average rate of almost 14 percent between 1973 and 1978 in the more prosperous cities, while revenues in the hard-pressed cities grew less than half as fast. Noneducational employment by city governments, including jobs supported by federal funds, grew by an average of 25 percent over this period in the cities classified as prosperous, while city employment declined by an average of 8 percent in the hard-pressed places.

Not surprisingly, these two groups of cities also showed substantial differences in the condition of their general funds. The condition of this fund can be measured in two ways. The first, shown in table 4, measures income to and expenditures from the general fund over the city fiscal year relative to total general fund expenditures. These figures indicate that the cities classified as hard pressed ran larger and more frequent revenue deficiencies over this period than more prosperous places. All of the hard-pressed cities were in deficit at least twice over this period, and three of them raised less than they spent in three or more years. The average deficiency was almost 6 percent of general fund expenditures. While all but one of the cities classified as more prosperous showed revenue deficiencies in at least two years, only Phoenix showed a deficiency in three or more years, and the aver-

Table 4. *General Fund Revenue Excess or Deficit*
as Percentage of General Fund Expenditures, 1973-78

City	1973	1974	1975	1976	1977	1978
	HARD-PRESSED CITIES					
New York	(7.2)	(15.6)	NA	(28.2)	(26.8)	(8.0)
Detroit	11.2	1.4	(4.5)	(3.1)	9.3	(3.6)
Cleveland[a]	NA	(0.1)	0.2	0.1	(0.2)	NA
Boston	NA	NA	(0.6)	(9.0)	(3.9)	(2.3)
St. Louis	(4.0)	(6.3)	8.5	1.4	1.1	2.7
	MORE PROSPEROUS CITIES					
Chicago	7.4	7.4	(0.1)	0.5	2.7	(2.0)
Los Angeles	(2.3)	10.1	2.2	2.1	0.3	5.2
Houston	(3.9)	6.0	3.2	1.4	1.7	(3.0)
Phoenix	(0.8)	(3.1)	(0.7)	2.3	3.7	(0.5)

Sources: Philip M. Dearborn, *Elements of Municipal Financial Analysis:*
Parts I-V (Boston: First Boston Corporation, 1975), and "The Financial Health of
Major U.S. Cities in 1978" (Washington, D.C.: The Urban Institute, Working Paper,
1979), and unpublished data. Comparable information was not available for Tulsa
or Rochester.

Note: Deficits are shown in parentheses.

a. As reported. Subsequent audits have indicated larger deficits.

age size of these deficiencies was less than half that of the hard-
pressed cities.

The second way to judge the condition of city general funds is
to measure the fund's surplus or deficit at the end of each fiscal
year. A current-year deficiency may be the result of unanticipated
revenue shortfalls or increased expenditures and not be a symp-
tom of any major problem if the government has an adequate level
of current assets available as a budget reserve. Table 5 displays the
difference between general fund assets (such as cash and invest-
ments) and liabilities (such as outstanding debts) for each city,
again expressed as a percentage of general fund expenditures.
Because these cities vary widely in the types of holdings they can
count as assets, balances and deficits have been recalculated on a
pro forma cash basis, which adjusts for the way these cities handle
assets.

The cities classified here as hard pressed showed larger and
more frequent deficits on this measure than the cities rated as
more prosperous. The only city in the latter group that showed
any general fund deficit—Chicago—did so because of state
accounting requirements for handling property taxes rather than

Table 5. *General Fund Surplus or Deficit as Percentage of General Fund Expenditures, 1973–78*
(pro forma cash basis)

City	1973	1974	1975	1976	1977	1978
HARD-PRESSED CITIES						
New York	(7.2)	(16.6)	NA	(28.2)	(26.8)	(8.1)
Detroit	4.4	4.4	0.1	(5.5)	4.0	(4.2)
Cleveland	0.1	—	0.1	0.3	0.1	NA
Boston	NA	NA	(0.4)	(4.7)	(4.5)	(9.5)
St. Louis	(2.8)	(8.6)	(0.2)	1.2	0.1	2.9
MORE PROSPEROUS CITIES						
Chicago	(36.0)	(29.0)	(25.0)	(24.9)	(21.2)	(22.6)
Los Angeles	23.5	39.6	27.0	21.5	17.7	22.4
Houston	3.3	6.3	7.6	7.5	8.4	3.8
Phoenix	4.7	0.5	1.5	3.0	8.3	9.5

Sources: Philip Dearborn, *Elements of Municipal Financial Analysis: Parts I-V* (Boston: First Boston Corporation, 1975), and "The Financial Health of Major U.S. Cities in 1978" (Washington, D.C.: The Urban Institute, Working Paper, 1979), and unpublished data.

Note: Deficits are shown in parentheses.

because of any severe financial problems.[3] Not only do the cities classified as hard pressed run more frequent deficits on a current-year basis, but they are also less well protected from potential adverse developments such as economic downturns or unanticipated expenditures.

If the argument here is correct, these two groups of cities should have used federal money for different purposes. Cities classified as prosperous might be expected to use limited amounts of federal dollars to support ongoing city activities, preferring instead to concentrate these funds in activities that could be easily terminated if federal funds were discontinued. In cities classified as hard pressed, federal funds should support a larger share of the city budget in general, and of basic city services in particular. In brief, the hard-pressed cities should be more politically and financially dependent on federal funds.

3. For a more detailed discussion of this problem, see Philip Dearborn, "The Financial Health of Major U.S. Cities in 1978" (Washington, D.C.: The Urban Institute, Working Paper, 1979).

Three Levels of Dependence

These three factors—financial condition, discretion, and levels of political organization and activity—divide the cities under consideration into three groups reflecting differences in political and financial dependence. The first group of cities is those classified as hard pressed. In these cities, all three factors create strong incentives for federal funds to be allocated through normal budgetary channels and for substantial amounts of these funds to be used to support basic city services. In the second group of cities—Chicago and Los Angeles—fiscal pressure has been less, but city discretion in the use of federal dollars has been high, and political conditions are such that one might expect a high level of conflict surrounding the allocation of federal funds and a fairly wide distribution of the benefits from federal dollars.

In the third group—Phoenix, Houston, and Tulsa—federal funds should be allocated more or less separately from other local revenues and should have minimal impact on local budgets. Because these cities are in strong financial condition, have little discretion in what to do with federal money, and have relatively inactive political systems, local officials have a strong incentive to adopt a conservative strategy in dealing with federal grants and avoid using them to support ongoing city services.

The next sections of this essay report on the differences among these three sets of cities in the political process surrounding the allocation of federal funds and the uses to which these dollars have been put—in short, on the differences in dependence.

Politics of Allocation

In the cities classified as hard pressed, the politics of allocating federal funds have become closely integrated with other forms of local politics. Because federal funds have become a major source of discretionary revenue in the budgets of most of these cities over this period, local officials, particularly mayors and councils, have had a strong incentive to assert control over these funds, both as a source of support for normal city activities and as a potential source of political capital.

This incentive has been strengthened further by the discretion available to these cities in where to spend federal money and by the level of political organization among the constituents of federally supported programs. Because relatively large areas of these cities are eligible to receive federal support, the number of elected officials, particularly council members, with a political stake in the

allocation of federal funds has expanded substantially over the last
ten years. As Henry Schmandt, George Wendel, and E. Allan
Tomey note of St. Louis:

Earlier grants—urban renewal, antipoverty, and model cities—were categorical
and the restrictions on their use provided little incentive for most aldermen to
become seriously involved. . . . Only in the case of model cities was the board in a
formal position to influence the distributional process, but relatively few of its
members were interested in intervening because the direct benefits were confined
to a small geographic area. In most cases, only the aldermen in the model cities
neighborhoods were likely to be actively concerned with the allocation of funds. . . .
More recently, the geographic distribution of federal funds, particularly CDBG, has
become the subject of much discussion. Black Northsiders complain that the white
South Side is favored in the allocation process, while community groups in the latter contend that the opposite is true. CDBG has become a battlefield issue in a
power struggle between the mayor and the Board of Aldermen.[8]

The constituents of federally supported programs are also well
organized and of some political consequence in these cities. All
five cities were active participants in the community development
and manpower programs of the 1960s. As a result, these functions
are not new to city government and the organizations and departments performing these functions have established stable constituencies with a strong interest in the way federal funds are
allocated. In addition, minority and neighborhood groups are well
established and organized, and are able to press demands for support through normal political channels rather than relying on citizen participation structures attached to the grants themselves.

Not surprisingly, programs supported by federal funds have
become major ingredients in mayoral electoral coalitions and
objects of constituent service by city councils. In Boston, New
York, and Detroit, mayors have been the major architects of such
federally funded coalitions as well as their principal political
beneficiaries. In Boston, for example, Jonathan Katz argues:

Mayor Kevin White and the city are committed to providing the social services that
depend on federal funds. The political power of the mayor is based to a great extent
on the support of recipients of social services and participants in housing, manpower, and economic development programs. Because civil service and strong
unions make the line agencies difficult for the mayor to control, improving the quality of their services is not easy and a political payoff in this area uncertain. Mayor
White has kept his distance from the line agencies, choosing instead to devote his
time to developing and publicizing the "second level of government" that federal
funds have made possible.[9]

8. Henry J. Schmandt, George D. Wendel, and E. Allan Tomey, *The Impact of
Federal Grants on the City of St. Louis* (Washington, D.C.: U.S. Departments of
Labor and Commerce, Report MEL 79-25(1), October 1979), p. 41.
    9. Jonathan Katz, *The Impact of Federal Grants on the City of Boston* (Wash-

A similar use of federal funds to develop and maintain a mayoral electoral coalition was noted in Detroit. As Thomas Anton notes:

Mayor Young has seen to it that substantial sums of money have poured into neighborhoods, particularly from the community development block grant, but from Community Service Administration and HEW grants as well. Substantial sums have been poured into neighborhood retail centers, housing, and service improvements all over the city. . . . The city has provided funds to some forty-three community organizations, including some that have been highly critical of the mayor in past years. . . . With a large and expanding network of neighborhood organizations who have benefited from their interactions with the mayor, a large pot of federal money to nourish this network, and a political style that is enormously popular with a largely black electorate, the mayor has created a base of electoral support that seems secure indeed.[10]

Councils in St. Louis and Cleveland have been particularly active in the allocation of federal funds, especially community development block grants. Mayors have generally been less powerful, both on paper and in practice, in these cities than in Detroit or Boston, and councils have been able to assert more control over the allocation of federal funds. In St. Louis, for example, Schmandt, Wendel, and Tomey note that the Board of Aldermen gained increased control over the allocation of CDBG funds after a conflict over the 1978 application. The board, which had been relatively uninvolved in earlier years, created procedural controls over the expenditure of CDBG funds and forced the reallocation of funds from downtown development, which the mayor had proposed, to neighborhood improvements and housing. The St. Louis authors argue that this initiative was largely the result of constituent pressure:

Initially, neighborhood groups had tended to work largely through the Community Development Agency machinery to obtain funds for their areas. When it became apparent, however, that the Citizen's Advisory Board—and even the CDA commission itself—lacked delivery power, community-based organizations began to turn to more traditional politics, pressuring their aldermanic representative to look after their interests.[11]

In brief, the politics surrounding the allocation of federal money in the cities classified as fiscally hard pressed is much like

---

ington, D.C.: U.S. Departments of Labor and Commerce, Report MEL 80-15, October 1980), p. 76.

10. Thomas J. Anton, *The Impact of Federal Grants on the City of Detroit in 1978* (Washington, D.C.: U.S. Departments of Labor and Commerce, Report MEL 81-11, June 1981), pp. 57-58.

11. Schmandt, Wendel, and Tomey, *St. Louis*, p. 47.

other local politics. Involvement by elected officials is substantial, and the constituents of federal funds press demands for funding through much the same channels, in the same way that they press demands for other city services.

A similar pattern appears in Chicago and Los Angeles, but with a slightly different focus. Neither of these places was under severe financial pressure over the period under consideration, and both went to considerable pains to keep federal funds out of basic city services and local funds out of the program areas supported with federal dollars. Like the earlier group of cities, however, both have considerable discretion in where they can spend federal money and both manifest organized and active political environments in which federal funds are allocated. These two factors have led to the creation of a "federal program arena," independent of the local budgetary process but involving the same decision makers and interest groups that are active in other local politics.[12]

The precise nature of this "federal arena" differs drastically, of course, between these two cities. In Chicago, Charles Orlebeke argues that the actors who allocate federal funds—the mayor and a relatively small set of upper-level city bureaucrats—do so in roughly the same fashion and in response to the same set of political pressures that influence the distribution of other city services:

Although Chicago's political executives—the mayor and key department heads—have had the most to say about the use of federal aid, they must function in a complex political environment and be sensitive to a variety of competing demands. Chicago politics is a balancing act rather than a dictatorship. Aldermen, ward committeemen, and other functionaries loyal to the machine expect a reasonable cut of all available resources, including federal funds; often pitted against the machine are neighborhood groups, citywide civic associations, watch-dog groups, environmentalists, civil rights groups, and public interest lawyers. During the Daley era, the city's executives managed both to keep the machine satisfied and to prevent its opponents—sometimes by making concessions—from seriously threatening its hegemony.[13]

Things are different in Los Angeles. Ruth Ross argues that the city's decentralized political system creates strong pressures on each city council member to develop an independent electoral coalition that will keep him or her in office. Community organiza-

12. This concept is taken from Pressman, *Federal Programs*.
13. Charles J. Orlebeke, *The Impact of Federal Grants on the City of Chicago* (Washington, D.C.: U.S. Departments of Labor and Commerce, Report MEL 80-11, April 1980), p. 91. For a detailed account of the bargaining surrounding the first two years of the CDBG program in Chicago that illustrates this general argument, see Leonard Rubinowitz, "Chicago," in Paul R. Dommel and associates, *Decentralizing Urban Policy* (Washington, D.C.: Brookings Institution, 1982).

tions interested in getting federal money are important elements
of these coalitions:

The most significant political influence of federal programs is the impact of citizen
participation requirements in the block grants. As a result of the social funding
coming into the city, community groups have gained experience at manipulating
the levers of power. The council grants committee and the full council make final
decisions about the use of federal funds, but only after intense lobbying from community groups. . . . [As a result of this lobbying] among the most politically successful programs funded with federal money are those of community groups that draw
on both CETA and CDBG. These programs are labor intensive, need little lead
time, and meet local demands. From the point of view of city council members, use
of CDBG and CETA money in this way provides constituent programs that are
popular with major voting blocks. At election time, council members can prove
they were responsive, but at limited direct cost to the regular city tax base.[14]

The allocation of federal dollars in these cities, in brief, takes
place outside the local budget but not outside the local political
system. While these cities face few demands to use federal funds
for ongoing city services, both cities have substantial discretion in
what they can use federal funds to support and politically important groups put considerable demands on these funds. Under
these conditions, federal funds constitute a substantial political
resource that local officials have some incentive to control and use
to advance their interests.

In comparison with the first two groups of cities, Houston,
Phoenix, and Tulsa separate the allocation of federal dollars from
city politics to a much greater degree. Because these cities are in
relatively strong financial condition, they have little incentive to
use federal funds to subsidize city operations. Further, small areas
of these cities are eligible to receive federal funds, minimizing the
number of elected officials with a political interest in how federal
funds are allocated. In addition, the beneficiaries of federal funds
are relatively unorganized, making it difficult for them to press
demands through normal political channels. These cities were
relatively inactive in the categorical programs of the 1960s, and
forms of political organization such as political parties are weak.
Finally, elected officials in these cities wish to avoid establishing
any continuing claims on local revenues by the constituents of
programs supported by federal funds. As a result, city officials have
little incentive to involve themselves in decisions about the use
of federal funds, and have generally ceded control over these
dollars to professional staff and concerned private groups.

14. Ruth Ross, *The Impact of Federal Grants on the City of Los Angeles* (Washington, D.C.: U.S. Departments of Labor and Commerce, Report MEL 80-21,
November 1980), pp. 69, 56-57, 71.

In Houston, for example, Susan MacManus notes that federally funded programs have been segregated, both financially and politically, from the normal city budget, and their allocation left mostly to program staff:

The CETA and Community Development divisions are not only fiscally but physically separate from city hall. . . . The city has solicited federal grants for social service programs, but has kept these federal dollars, and city personnel supported by these dollars, separate from the city's general fund budget. . . . By and large, Houston's elected officials have played a minor role in decisions about the use of federal funds. The only impact city officials have had has been through their appointments to departments and divisions receiving substantial federal aid. . . . Administrators have solicited input from the mayor and various council members, but quietly and privately.[15]

The operation of the allocation process in Tulsa was described in similar terms:

The Board of Commissioners generally approves the annual budget (which includes grants for city agencies) with very little fanfare since the substantive debates precede the commission's review. . . . The budget is primarily prepared by specialists in a decentralized format, defended by specialists, and approved by a city commission that has neither the power nor the inclination to enforce overall planning and coordination.[16]

These three cities present examples of risk aversion in dealing with federal dollars. Because they are under little fiscal pressure, they have little incentive to use federal funds as a source of support for normal city activity. Unlike officials in Chicago and Los Angeles, elected officials in these cities have little incentive to use federal dollars as a source of political capital outside the city budget. These officials have relatively little discretion in where federal funds can be spent and confront relatively few active political demands for these funds, so they have equally limited incentives to invest substantial time or effort exercising political control over these programs and have delegated their operation largely to program staffs.

In brief, there is substantial variation in the political importance of federal funds in the eleven cities studied. In cities that have some discretion in deciding how to spend federal dollars and that have politically significant groups interested in their use,

15. Susan A. MacManus, *The Impact of Federal Grants on the City of Houston* (Washington, D.C.: U.S. Departments of Labor and Commerce, Report MEL 79-25(2), November 1979), p. 27.

16. Steve B. Steib and R. Lynn Rittenoure, *The Impact of Federal Grants on the City of Tulsa* (Washington, D.C.: U.S. Departments of Labor and Commerce, Report MEL 80-05, March 1980), p. 56.

elected city officials have had some incentive to gain control of the allocation of these programs and use them as political resources in much the same fashion, and to much the same ends, as other resources. In cities where both discretion and potential political gain have been lacking, officials have directed their attention elsewhere.

4. Consequences of Differences in Dependence

The differences in the degree to which cities are fiscally and politically dependent on federal funds have two main consequences. The first is seen in differences in the types of services cities have used federal money to support, which should be more closely tied to city fiscal pressure than to city politics. The second is seen in differences in the way benefits from federal funds are distributed among different income groups, which should be more responsive to variations in local discretion and political conditions. This section examines these two types of consequences.

Functional Use of Federal Funds

For a variety of reasons, cities under fiscal pressure use federal dollars for different purposes—purposes that make them more dependent on federal aid—than cities with less trouble balancing their budgets. In particular, hard-pressed cities use substantial amounts of federal money to support ongoing city activities, particularly "basic" services such as police, fire, and streets. More prosperous cities, by contrast, try to avoid using federal funds for these purposes, using them instead in service areas that are not essential to ongoing city operations or that could be terminated without establishing any claim on the city budget.

As table 6 shows, the cities classified as hard pressed allocated almost half of federal funds used for operating purposes to support "basic" services, compared with less than one-fifth for the more prosperous cities. Federal funds supported an average of more than 20 percent of city operating expenditures for these services in the hard-pressed places, compared with less than 10 percent in less distressed cities. Clearly, over this period at any rate, the

Table 6. *Federal Support for Basic Services, Operating Programs, by Financial Condition*

City	Percentage of federal funds spent on basic services	Federal spending as percentage of total spending for basic services
HARD-PRESSED CITIES		
Detroit[a]	49.0	25.5
St. Louis[a]	49.9	27.0
Cleveland	46.0	24.0
Rochester	92.4	22.3
New York[b]	55.3	22.7
Boston	39.3	13.0
Average, hard-pressed cities	54.2	21.2
MORE PROSPEROUS CITIES		
Houston	16.5	4.4
Phoenix	30.2	14.7
Tulsa	18.3	11.3
Chicago	28.7	10.9
Los Angeles	10.3	4.5
Average, more prosperous cities	20.5	9.1

Source: Case study reports.

Note: Basic services include public safety, public works, sanitation, and general administration. For New York and Boston, schools have also been included. See text for details.

a. Estimated on basis of employment.

b. Excludes AFDC and medicaid.

hard-pressed cities were more dependent than more prosperous cities on federal funds to maintain basic services.

The substantial use of federal funds by the hard-pressed cities, to support basic services appears to reflect more or less explicit decisions to insulate basic service departments from the consequences of city financial difficulties by using federal dollars to maintain their operations. In Cleveland, for example, where federal funds supported more than 25 percent of city spending for public safety, Richard Tompkins argues:

A charter change in 1968 required that police in Cleveland be paid a wage at least 3 percent higher than the highest police wage in other large Ohio cities. . . . In addition to these pressures of increasing costs, it has been the policy of several administrations to insulate the police department from personnel layoffs because most political leaders felt the electorate would not stand for a reduction in police services. As a result of these two factors, Cleveland has relied heavily on multiple sources of federal funds to supplement limited increases in local revenue. PSE, CDBG, and [Economic Development Administration] funds, as well as [Law Enforcement Assistance Administration], revenue sharing, and [antirecession fiscal assistance] funds have been used to support police activities.[1]

Similar decisions were reported in other cities. In Rochester, for example, Sarah Liebschutz reports that growing uncontrollable costs, largely for employee pensions, led local officials to cut local employment by 18 percent between 1973 and 1978. They did so largely by transferring functions to the overlying county government or to private contractors. The only departments exempt from this reduction were police and fire, which made up half of all full-time employees in 1978.

In Detroit, Anton argues that the strength of municipal employee unions, particularly the police, has been responsible for city use of federal funds to support basic city services:

Part of the reason why more city jobs have not been eliminated has been the strong mutuality of interest between city agencies, reluctant to abandon established service commitments, and municipal employee unions, reluctant to lose jobs. This mutuality of interest, together with increasing militancy on the part of union leaders faced with apparently continuous budget crises, has in fact achieved very favorable results for city workers, imposing significant cost increases even without personnel increases. The significance of outside aid for these generously paid city workers is substantial. Federal dollars were used in 1978 to support virtually all city activities: only seven of the forty-five city agencies budgeted no federally supported positions in that year. Manpower, Neighborhood Services, and Planning were supported entirely by federal dollars, while traditionally city services such as police and fire, recreation, and environmental maintenance were carried out by large numbers of employees paid from federal funds.[2]

St. Louis's use of federal funds was shaped by a slightly different set of political factors. The city has no control over its police expenditures, which are set by a state board appointed by the governor, on which the mayor is the only city representative. Because the city is required to support the police department from its own funds at the level set by this board, it has little incentive to use federal funds to support this service. Instead, it has concentrated federal funds heavily in general government and streets, which draw about one-third of their budgets from federal dollars.

By contrast, the more prosperous cities adopted relatively explicit policies to minimize the potential consequences to the

1. Richard F. Tompkins *et al.*, *The Impact of Federal Grants on the City of Cleveland* (Washington, D.C.: U.S. Departments of Labor and Commerce, Report MEL 81-19, February 1981), pp. 8, 29-30.
2. Anton, *Detroit*, p. 39.

city budget if federal funds were discontinued. Three such policies can be noted.

The first is to use federal dollars in basic service departments only to support activities that could be easily discontinued if federal dollars were cut. In general, these cities are even less reliant on federal funds to support basic services than the figures in table 4 suggest, since much of the spending these figures reflect supported modest expansions of service or one-time projects rather than normal operations. Such programs include expansion of street maintenance, police-community relations programs, fire surveys, or other activities not directly involved in police patrol or fighting fires. This pattern was particularly marked in the activities supported by public service employment funds. Chicago, for example, used substantial amounts of PSE funds to support basic service departments, but Orlebeke argues that these funds largely supported program expansion:

The city saw PSE as an opportunity to start new programs or expand others, with the federal government picking up most of the tab. For example, the Police Department used federal funds to hire over 100 Spanish-speaking public safety aides. The Fire Department used PSE primarily to develop its elite Mobile Intensive Care Units; CETA funds covered about 200 drivers and attendants eligible for paramedic training, who could move into paramedic vacancies as they occurred.[3]

Los Angeles used PSE funds in similar fashion. Ross notes that PSE funds supported activities in such departments as public works and traffic that could be terminated without affecting the delivery of services:

Even though PSE workers were a significant part of the total work force in these departments, in general they performed functions that could easily be cut back with little harm to basic city services. From the city government's point of view, PSE allowed it to tidy up public facilities, supplement cultural activities, and catch up on the bureaucracy's paper work.[4]

The only exception to this general pattern was Phoenix, which is subject to a state law that limits growth in expenditures financed by local sources, but that does not apply to expenditures financed by federal grants. John Hall argues that Phoenix budget officials used this loophole to finance a substantial expansion of basic services through use of federal funds, largely general revenue sharing and PSE funds.

The second major policy followed by more prosperous governments to minimize the consequences of reductions in federal

3. Orlebeke, *Chicago,* pp. 46-47.
4. Ross, *Los Angeles,* p. 39.

funds has been to avoid using local money for the activities that
federal dollars support, in order to minimize potential claims on
local dollars if federal funds are discontinued. Most human service
activities in these cities are almost totally supported with federal
funds. In Tulsa, for example, Steib and Rittenoure note:

City and county departments and trusts contribute a relatively small share of locally
raised revenue to social services and to programs that pursue social goals. This
situation not only reflects the prevailing sentiment of political leaders, but also the
city charter which states that the city has "no welfare responsibility." Similarly,
city agencies usually use federal money designated for capital improvements in
low-income neighborhoods for projects that do not require local agencies to spend
money for future operation and upkeep.[5]

Finally, more prosperous governments actively pursue funds
from federal capital programs for roads, sewers, subways, and
other physical facilities. Although Congress can change authoriza-
tions and appropriations for capital programs as readily as for operating programs, capital grants are generally made on a "full
funding" basis—under which the federal agency making the grant
sets aside the total federal share of a project's cost when the award
is made. This practice minimizes the uncertainty associated with
federal capital dollars. The more prosperous cities see capital
funds as a way to expand services to keep pace with population
growth or to enhance economic development without incurring
local debt, thereby keeping local taxes down. Federal capital programs accounted for approximately the same share of city capital
spending in more prosperous cities as in poor ones. Spending
from federal capital programs in 1978 was the equivalent of about
half of average capital spending over the previous three years in
rich and poor cities alike.

Economic Stimulus Package

Although in general hard-pressed cities used federal dollars to
support different types of services from the more prosperous cities,
this difference did not appear in all federal grants. In particular,
cities did not differ appreciably in the ways they spent the largest
source of new federal dollars they received in fiscal 1978—the
Carter administration's economic stimulus package programs.

The stimulus package was Carter's response to the lingering
effects of the economic recession of 1973 to 1975. Much of the
stimulus spending occurred during fiscal year 1978, which began

5. Steib and Rittenoure, *Tulsa*, p. 33.

in October 1977. The primary source of new federal dollars received by cities in fiscal 1978 came through two major components of the stimulus package: (1) an expansion of title VI of the public service employment (PSE) program, designed to provide temporary jobs for those unemployed because of the recession, and (2) the local public works (LPW) program, designed to stimulate employment in the construction industry.[6] Hard-pressed and more prosperous cities used these federal funds in roughly the same ways.

This similarity is particularly marked in the use of PSE funds. During fiscal 1978, the PSE program was funded with money authorized under two titles of the Comprehensive Employment and Training Act: title VI, the countercyclical portion, and title II, which was intended for persons who had been unemployed for long periods. Because title VI was seen as a temporary measure, Congress required localities to use title VI funds for special projects that could be completed within one year. Title VI is often referred to as the "project" portion of PSE. Title II, by contrast, was more permanent and could be used to sustain the levels of public services that governments had been able to provide in the past; this title was thus known as the "sustainment" portion.

No matter what their fiscal condition, cities followed similar patterns in their uses of funds under the two PSE titles. Two practices are particularly worthy of note.

First, cities retained a large portion of sustainment positions for assignment to their own government agencies, but assigned large proportions of project positions to other governments or to nonprofit organizations. About two-thirds of all sustainment positions were retained on city payrolls; hard-pressed cities retained in excess of 80 percent of these positions. With the exception of Cleveland, which was approaching default during this period, fewer than 40 percent of all project slots were retained on city pay-

6. Both these programs were expansions or reauthorizations of already existing programs that differed in a number of ways from earlier versions. For descriptions of these differences in LPW, see U.S. Commerce Department, Economic Development Administration, *Local Public Works Program: Status Report* (Washington, D.C.: U.S. Government Printing Office, 1978). For a more complete description of the PSE program, see Richard P. Nathan *et al., Public Service Employment: A Field Evaluation* (Washington, D.C.: Brookings Institution, 1981). The third part of the stimulus package, the antirecession fiscal assistance (ARFA) program, is not considered here because several of the more prosperous places received only negligible allocations, making comparisons difficult.

rolls and the difference between hard-pressed and more prosperous cities was small.

Second, both groups of cities used large numbers of project
positions either to support social services (largely through subcon-
tracts with community organizations) or to expand such activities
as park maintenance and street cleaning, which could use relatively unskilled workers who could be put to work quickly. Some
cities used project funds to rehire some laid-off city workers, but
such uses were significantly less common than under the sustainment title.

These uses of project funds had two roots. First, it was simply
harder to use project funds to support normal operations than to
use sustainment funds for the same purposes. The eligibility
requirements for hiring were more restrictive than those under the
sustainment portion of the program, and there was a one-year limit
on the length of time an individual could occupy a project position,
but no such limit for sustainment positions. Finally, there was an
informal requirement that one-third of all project slots be subcon-
tracted to community organizations; no such requirement was
attached to sustainment funds.

Second, project funds were not likely to continue. The stimulus
package—which expanded the project portion more than the sustainment portion—was presented publicly as a one-time infusion
of funds rather than as a permanent new program, and there was
considerable public speculation that the project PSE funds might
be made part of the Carter administration's welfare reform program. Governments thus had little incentive to use project funds to
support normal operations.

This incentive was weakened further by the relative improvement in the financial condition of most of the hard-pressed cities
between 1976, when local economies were still affected by the
1973–75 recession, and 1977, when most had recovered. Both
Detroit and Boston, for example, moved from general fund revenue deficits in 1976 to revenue excesses in 1977, and New York's
revenue deficit was over $100 million lower in 1977 than in
1976.[7]

Differences between hard-pressed and more prosperous cities
in the use of local public works funds were more substantial. LPW

---

7. For a detailed assessment of the financial conditions of these cities over this
period, see Philip M. Dearborn, *The Financial Health of Major U.S. Cities in 1977*
(Boston: First Boston Corporation, 1978).

was a more significant portion of the capital budgets of harder pressed cities than of less distressed ones. On the average among the hard-pressed cities studied, LPW allocations received during 1978 accounted for 21 percent of an average year's capital spending (as calculated from figures for the previous three years). The comparable figure was 13 percent in the more prosperous places.

Hard-pressed cities also more frequently used LPW funds to support renovation and rehabilitation. Typical LPW projects in poorer cities were relatively small projects such as street and sidewalk reconstruction and repair or renovation of public facilities that had been postponed in the past due to financial problems. In several cities, the backlog of such projects had grown to considerable size as a result of earlier reductions in borrowing and maintenance expenditures. In Boston, for example,

Part of the city's success in launching the LPW program can be attributed to the abundance of already planned capital projects that had been delayed for lack of funds. The requirement that LPW projects have workers on the job in 90 days precluded the funding of any new projects. . . . However, the requirement actually suited the city's situation, because many capital projects were on the shelf, most having the necessary design work and approvals already in place. These projects had been passed over in the CDBG budget and the capital budget, which had earlier been curtailed because of fiscal constraints.[8]

Attempts to link LPW funds with other economic development efforts appear to have been more the exception than the rule, although during this period several cities were undertaking substantial downtown redevelopment campaigns, which LPW could have been used to support. Only in Detroit and Chicago were substantial amounts of LPW funds successfully plugged into ongoing economic development efforts, particularly downtown projects. Cleveland also tried to use LPW funds as a part of larger plans for downtown development, but had considerable legal and political difficulties in implementing these plans. In other cities, the program's emphasis on projects that could be started quickly, a maximum limit on federal support for any single project, and an emphasis by federal agencies on projects that would create large numbers of jobs led cities to tilt project selection toward smaller projects that could be begun relatively quickly and to look for other funding for larger projects.[9] Thus, in Los Angeles, Ruth

8. Katz, *Boston*, p. 34.

9. LPW funds were granted in two rounds, the first in winter 1977 and the second in fall 1977. In the first, the Economic Development Administration selected projects from applications submitted by local governments. In the second round,

Ross reports the following:

When LPW was passed, the city submitted 212 projects from its backlog of second-priority capital improvement projects. The federal government funded 34 in round one for a total of $26.5 million. When round two regulations were amended to permit the city to select projects, a top priority was the Piper Technical Center. The city wanted to concentrate the money, but EDA wanted projects that could be completed more quickly and rejected it. The city subsequently set up a nonprofit corporation to build the technical center, and council members then chose from the remaining LPW projects based on their district's needs. Members essentially conducted a round robin, selecting one project per district until the money was allocated.[10]

In sum, several factors reduced the incentive of cities to attempt to use PSE funds to support normal city operations or to integrate LPW funds with larger economic development efforts. These factors include federal agency pressures to obligate and spend large amounts of money in a short period of time, program features designed to increase the rate at which funds were spent, uncertainty about future funding, and short-term improvements in cities' fiscal condition. Dependence on stimulus funds, even among the hard-pressed cities, was generally far less than on other federal dollars.

Distribution of Benefits from Federal Funds

Because grant dollars subsidize general operations in harder-pressed cities and the politics surrounding the allocation of these dollars has been more intense, the benefits from federally funded programs have been more broadly dispersed than in the more prosperous cities, where benefits have been more concentrated among lower-income groups. These differences in benefits have been particularly marked in CDBG and CETA. These block grants were intended to provide services to lower-income groups but also provide local governments with substantial discretion in how funds are to be used.

Table 7 presents estimates of the fraction of expenditures from CDBG, the PSE portion of CETA, and all federal funds that benefited low- and moderate-income groups in each city in 1978. The income groups are defined by reference to city median income. "Low income" is defined as 50 percent or less of the median income of families in the city, and "moderate income" as between 50 and 80 percent of the city median. Benefits from federal pro-

local governments were allowed to choose projects to be funded from applications already on file.

10. Ross, *Los Angeles*, pp. 36-37.

Table 7. *Percentage of Federal Grant Expenditures Benefiting Low- and Moderate-Income Groups, 1978*

City	Community development block grants[a]	Public service employment[b]	All federal grants
	HARD-PRESSED CITIES		
Detroit	47	32	59
Cleveland	35	33	55
Rochester	68	82	62
Boston	30	81	NA
St. Louis	37	91	76
Average	43	63	63
	MORE PROSPEROUS CITIES		
Phoenix	93	85	88
Los Angeles	52	100	91
Tulsa	54	100	52
Chicago	76	100	73
Average	69	96	76

Source: Case study reports.

Note: Income groups are defined by reference to city median family income. "Low income" indicates income less than 50 percent of city median; "moderate income" indicates income between 50 and 80 percent of city median. Comparable data were not available for New York or Houston.

a. Benefits defined by income composition of the area where activities supported by CDBG funds were located.

b. Benefits defined by characteristics of individuals paid with PSE funds.

grams were allocated in a number of ways. The benefits from capital projects, such as those funded by CDBG or LPW funds, were allocated on the basis of the income of the area where the projects were located. The income incidence of service programs such as PSE or child nutrition was determined by the characteristics of service recipients. The benefits from such programs as downtown development or general revenue sharing, which can be argued to benefit the population as a whole, were allocated on the basis of the proportion of each income group in the total population. The figures in the table should be viewed as approximations, since they are based in many cases on 1970 income data and on planned rather than actual expenditures. They do, however, provide a rough indication of which groups are the primary beneficiaries of federal funds.

On average, low- and moderate-income groups were the primary beneficiaries of more than three-quarters of federally supported expenditures in more prosperous cities, compared with about three-fifths of such expenditures in harder-pressed cities. The share of CDBG and PSE expenditures that benefited lower-income groups in the more properous cities was almost one-and-a-half times larger than in the poorer ones. Judged on the basis of project location, lower-income groups in the more prosperous cities were the beneficiaries of over 75 percent of CDBG expenditures, compared with less than 50 percent in the hard-pressed cities. The disparity in the income levels of PSE participants was almost as large. Almost 100 percent of PSE participants were members of lower-income groups in more prosperous cities, compared with less than two-thirds of participants in hard-pressed cities.

This disparity in the beneficiaries of federal funds can be traced to several sources, most of which have already been discussed. First, the hard-pressed cities had more discretion in spending federal dollars. Regulations for the community development block grant constrained them less than the more prosperous places, and it was relatively easy for them to convert "sustainment" PSE funds into a source of support for general city activities. Second, they had more incentive to use this discretion. Because they were unable to support ongoing city services at politically acceptable levels from local revenue, they had a considerable incentive to use federal funds to support normal city services, which benefit the entire city population. Officials in these cities also had a considerable incentive to use these funds as political resources, leading them to "spread" benefits rather than focusing them in the poorest areas of the city.

The politics of this spreading process varied among cities. In New York, Boston, and Detroit, mayors used federal funds as a way to develop and maintain political support. In New York, Julia Vitullo-Martin argues that the city's tendency to spread the benefits occurred as a result of two factors. One was increased demands on these funds from middle-income areas, accentuated by a city charter that mandates formal citizen participation in the allocation of funds. The second was administrative pressure to implement programs quickly, which tends to favor programs benefiting moderate- and middle-income areas. She argues further that the ability to allocate funds to a wide range of areas strengthened the mayor's position in responding to these demands.

Federal funds help the mayor out, since he controls the money and can distribute CDBG and employment money and contracts to the boroughs. There's enough poverty and dilapidated housing to go around, so the mayor can easily choose to favor some boroughs over others without violating federal regulations. At the same time, he can always call on federal regs to justify denying aid to others.[11]

In Boston, Katz argues that the city has followed a more explicit strategy of dispersing funds as widely as possible:

In distributing the jobs and services funded by federal aid programs, city officials try to provide something for everyone. Many decisions on how to allocate federal funds concentrate on spending something in each of the city's neighborhoods. Because the city's largest political constituency is its middle income residents, officials make sure they obtain some benefits. . . . Under this distribution strategy, growing numbers of city residents are receiving services and expect them to continue. There are obvious political benefits for an administration to pursue this policy which actively reaches out to a broader constituency.[12]

By contrast, pressures for spreading funds in Cleveland and St. Louis came largely from the city council and were largely centered around community development funds. In Cleveland, Tompkins argues that social service agencies and mayors as well as the council have seen the potential political benefits of spreading federal funds. Council members seek benefits for their wards; social service agencies seek funds to support their activities; mayors have a strong interest in using federal funds to support normal citywide operations. As a result of these common interests, almost 75 percent of the city was defined as eligible for community development projects. This area was narrowed to 40 percent in 1978 as a result of pressure from HUD, community groups, and the community development director, but Tompkins argues that the pressures from the council for dispersal of funds remain substantial:

Despite these efforts, almost half of the 1978 CDBG expenditures were for services dispersed throughout the city such as public safety, environmental health, and programs delivered by non-profit social service agencies. Programs targeted towards neighborhoods continued to be subject to three separate council approvals and the accompanying political considerations.[13]

The major form of spreading the benefits of PSE funds has been their use to rehire laid-off city workers, as was done extensively in New York, Cleveland, and Detroit. New York, for example, rehired approximately 2,500 policemen and sanitation and park workers using PSE funds, while Detroit rehired several hundred policemen.

The richer cities are more complex. In Phoenix, Houston, and Tulsa, there was relatively little incentive to spread federal dollars

---

11. Julia Vitullo-Martin, "The Impact of Federal Grants on New York City, FY 1972-FY 1978" (processed, May 1981), p. 91.

12. Katz, *Boston*, p. 81.

13. Tompkins *et al.*, *Cleveland*, p. 62.

for any reason. Because these cities have little discretion in where to spend federal money, fewer elected officials are in a position to claim political credit for the uses of federal money. In similar fashion, there is little incentive to use federal funds as a source of support for normal city operations. These conditions have strengthened the bargaining position of program staff and others interested in targeting funds on lower-income areas. In Phoenix, for example, John Hall argues that the concentration of federal funds in South Phoenix is the result of both local political conditions and federal pressure:

A local coalition concerned about the general deterioration of the area and particularly its housing problems has, until recently, been successful in selling CDBG as an act designed to benefit low and moderate income individuals. HUD has reinforced this interpretation by rejecting plans for parks and recreational facilities in more affluent parts of the city. . . . Although CDBG and other social agency targeting appear to stem from combined federal incentives and local politics, other targeting efforts are much more the direct result of federal formulas and regulations.[14]

In Chicago and Los Angeles, the situation has been more complicated, particularly with regard to CDBG. Because federal programs are important political resources in these cities, the politics surrounding their allocation have been more complex than in cities where decisions about federal money are largely left to staff. In Chicago, the city government's desire to disperse federal funds to as many neighborhoods as possible has conflicted with demands from neighborhood groups and the constituencies of the former model cities and community action agencies, who have been pushing the city to target funds. The situation has been further complicated by the political and legal maneuvering surrounding the implementation of the *Gautreaux* decision, in which a federal judge in 1969 ordered the city to locate subsidized housing outside of minority areas. Orlebeke argues that these forces together have compelled the city to concentrate an increasing amount of funds in low-income areas:

The city government and HUD have groped for an accommodation with each other, and with the city's contending political forces. [The attorney for the Gautreaux plaintiffs] and his allies submit detailed "administrative complaints" to HUD each year charging noncompliance with the city's housing assistance goals; neighborhood groups also go to HUD directly to complain. HUD has been very reluctant to intervene in the local CDBG planning process or to punish the city by cutting CDBG funds. The result has been that the city's CDBG planners maneuver and negotiate among neighborhood groups, civil rights organizations, social service agencies, and other interests in order to fashion the program each year. Although

14. Hall, *Phoenix*, p. 61.

HUD sometimes issues stern admonitions, in the end it has generally backed whatever plan the city comes up with. . . . It does appear that the combination of HUD pressure, political demands from neighborhood groups, and prevailing wisdom in urban planning—not necessarily in that order of importance—have moved Chicago's community development program towards the targeting objective.[15]

In Los Angeles, the main effect of political maneuvering around CDBG has been to produce a greater spreading of funds among income groups than in other prosperous cities. The city has no single clearly identifiable pocket of poverty within which funds have to be spent, and the city's decentralized political system encourages council members to pursue federal funds as a means of maintaining voter support.

Unless the federal government requires otherwise, the legislators prefer to split all federal grants (more or less equally) among the fifteen council districts. . . . Most council members have learned the political benefits of federal grants, especially such programs as CDBG and LPW. These programs enable council members to provide visible public improvements and social services for their constituencies at relatively little cost to the city treasury. . . . When the bargaining is over, almost every member gets some funds, regardless of whether the member's district has a large proportion of low and moderate income residents or not. In the first four years of the CDBG program, for example, each council district received at least some funds, although the districts with the lowest median income received the largest amounts of aid.[16]

15. Orlebeke, *Chicago*, pp. 88 and 101.
16. Ross, *Los Angeles*, pp. 1 and 56.

5. Conclusion

This analysis has identified three distinct patterns in federal aid's budgetary and political impact among the eleven cities under consideration. This section reviews those patterns and discusses the likely consequences of cutbacks in federal aid.

In the six cities classified as financially hard pressed, federal funds have become major sources of support for ongoing city activities, particularly basic services, and have become major sources of political capital for city officials. Federal funds were the fastest-growing source of city revenue over this period and local officials were unable to maintain politically acceptable levels of basic services from local revenues. As a result, mayors and budget officials made considerable use of federal funds to support such basic city services as police, fire, and sanitation, which might otherwise have been reduced. Federal funds were allocated through the same decision-making processes, and by the same actors, as other local revenues, and were spent in ways that resemble the ways in which locally raised dollars were spent.

The second major pattern appears in Chicago and Los Angeles, where federal funds have not been used to support basic city services, but have become integrated into local politics. During the mid-1970s, both these cities were in relatively strong financial condition, making it possible for city officials to follow a relatively cautious policy of segregating the activities supported by federal funds from those supported by local revenues. Federal funds were used to support activities in departments that provide basic services, but these activities have been nonrecurring expenditures or activities that could be discontinued with relatively little difficulty if federal funds were terminated. By the same token, officials in both these cities avoided committing local funds to human service activities supported primarily with federal dollars, in order to avoid creating any local liability for these programs.

In these two cities, however, the process of allocating federal funds has been closely tied to local politics, for much the same reasons as in the hard-pressed cities. Relatively large areas of these cities are eligible to receive federal funds, and program constituents are relatively well organized and politically important. Under these conditions, decisions on allocating federal aid are made by the same actors—the upper levels of department bureaucracies in Chicago and the city council in Los Angeles—and in response to much the same set of political demands and constraints as decisions on allocating local resources.

The third major pattern of federal aid use appears in Phoenix, Tulsa, and Houston, where federal funds have become neither a major source of support for normal city services nor an important political issue. Because these cities have been financially strong, they have generally kept federal funds segregated from local revenue and have avoided using grants to support ongoing city services. Instead, they have used federal funds largely to finance new services, such as manpower or community development, which they were not providing before federal support became available for these purposes. Federal dollars have also enabled these cities to provide capital facilities or expand services to keep pace with population growth without increasing local taxes.

By contrast with the situation in the first two sets of cities, federal funds have not become political issues in these three cities. Federal regulations have the effect of limiting the areas within which funds can be spent in these cities, and program constituents are less well organized and have less political power than in the other cities in this study. The allocation of federal dollars has not become a major concern of local elected officials, but has rather been largely determined by professional program staff and local service agencies.

Three points are particularly worthy of note. First, the amount of federal money a city receives—whether compared with its own revenues or judged against any other standard—has little relation to its dependence on these funds to support ongoing city services. Hard-pressed and more prosperous cities have used federal funds to support very different activities, but these differences are not reflected in the amount of federal money these two kinds of cities receive. According to the figures in table 3, the cities classified as prosperous are more "dependent" on federal money than the hard-pressed cities, because the federal aid they receive is larger relative to local taxes than the comparable figure for the hard-pressed cities.

Second, there is considerable variety in the politics surrounding the allocation of federal funds, and these different political conditions appear to influence the way federal aid is spent. In some cities, decisions about how to spend federal dollars are made primarily by elected officials, in others by professional staff. In cities where elected officials are the major decision makers, federal funds are more likely to be used to support basic services and to benefit the population at large than in places where professional staff have more to say about what is done with federal money. The presumption that federal money is allocated more or less the same in all cities and in response to the same set of forces that drives the allocation of local funds appears unwarranted, at least for this set of cities. Politics differ, and they cause spending patterns to differ as well.

Finally, the conditions surrounding grants, particularly the uncertainty of their continuation and the amount of discretion they provide local officials, appear to have a considerable effect on how cities spend federal dollars. In spite of the large amounts of money provided to these cities under the economic stimulus package, for example, both the uncertainty of continued support and federal agency pressure to spend money in particular ways appear to have led all but the most hard pressed of these cities to avoid using these funds to support ongoing city activities. In similar fashion, different degrees of discretion stemming from CDBG regulations appear to have produced different uses of these funds across these cities.[1]

The differences in dependence and in the politics surrounding the allocation of federal funds suggest that substantial reductions in grant programs will have a very different impact on these cities. The next section suggests some of these differences.

The Consequences of Cuts

As noted earlier, the case studies focused on the local political and budgetary response to a massive build-up in the level of fed-

1. For a more developed version of these latter two arguments, see V. Lane Rawlins and Richard P. Nathan, "The Field Network Evaluation Studies of Intergovernmental Grants: A Contrast with the Conventional Neoclassical Economic Approach," paper presented at the annual meeting of the American Economic Association, 1981.

eral grants for cities that occurred during the mid-1970s. In particular, these studies focus on federal aid received and spent in 1978,
which marked the high point of this support relative to both total
federal outlays and local revenues.

Since 1978, the federal aid picture has changed sharply. The
Carter administration's attempt to make the economic stimulus
package programs permanent was unsuccessful, and substantial
restrictions were imposed on the types of individuals who could
be hired under the PSE program, their tenure once hired, and the
maximum salaries they could be paid.[2] As a result of these and
other changes, the amount of federal support for cities leveled off
between 1978 and 1981. More recently, and more importantly,
major changes have been initiated by the Reagan administration.
Briefly, these changes fall into three major categories.[3]

The first has been a major reduction in the level of funding for
a large number of grant programs. Largely as a result of administration initiatives, federal support for state and local government
activities other than welfare declined substantially between 1981
and 1983. The PSE program was abolished in 1981, and substantial
reductions have been enacted in mass transit operation and construction, airport and sewer construction, economic development,
training and employment and a variety of education and social
service programs. While there have been significant increases in
welfare spending over this same period, so that total grant spending
has declined only slightly, federal support for other state and local
activities declined by over 11 percent between 1981 and 1983,
falling from $54.8 billion to $48.6 billion.

Further reductions have been proposed in the administration's
1984 budget, particularly in those grants that fund operating
programs. While construction grant spending is projected to grow
substantially as a result of increases in the federal gas tax, which
finances highway and mass transit construction, and the Emergency
Jobs Act adopted in early 1983, a variety of cuts have been proposed
in social services, economic development, and transportation pro-

2. For a more detailed description of these changes, see Nathan *et al., Public
Service Employment,* pp. 118-19.

3. For more detailed descriptions of the Reagan proposals, see John W. Ell-
wood, ed., *Reductions in U.S. Domestic Spending: How They Affect State and
Local Governments* (New Brunswick, N.J.: Transaction Books, 1982); and Edward
Gramlich, "Aid to State and Local Governments," in Joseph Pechman, ed., *Setting
National Priorities: The 1983 Budget* (Washington, D.C.: The Brookings Institu-
tion, 1982).

grams. Excluding capital programs and welfare, federal support for state and local operating programs is projected to decline to $26.7 billion in 1984, a reduction of 18 percent since 1981.

The second major change in the grant system stemming from Reagan administration initiatives has been the consolidation of a large number of categorical grant programs into block grants, generally to state governments. Eleven block grants, amounting to approximately $10 billion in outlays, have been created in the last two years, and the 1984 budget contains proposals for five additional programs for Indian community development and housing, aging, nutrition and education.

Third, and potentially more importantly, the administration has proposed to "turnback" the operations of a large number of grant programs to state and local governments. The 1983 budget contained an ambitious proposal to turnback some 125 programs, with approximately $45 billion in outlays, including all major urban aid to state governments, and to rearrange financial responsibility for major welfare programs. The 1984 budget contains a more modest proposal to consolidate 34 programs with annual outlays of $21 billion into three grants to state governments and one to local governments, which would have restrictions on the use of Community Development Block Grant funds removed over a period of five years. Neither turnback proposal has received any substantial political support, and any large scale reassignment of program or financial responsibility seems unlikely.

While a complete evaluation of the consequences of either enacted or proposed reductions is beyond the scope of this essay, it is possible to offer several general comments on the likely consequences of the budget cuts enacted in 1982–83 and proposed for 1984 in this set of cities.

First, the short-term consequences of the two budgets for cities in general, and for these cities in particular, may be limited. Most of the programs that absorbed the largest reductions in earlier budgets and were proposed to be reduced in fiscal 1984 do not provide substantial funds to city governments, although several do support services to city residents by special districts, such as transit authorities and school districts.[4] The reduction that most directly affected the city governments under consideration here in an

4. For an evaluation of the initial effects of the 1982 budget changes including most of the cities reported here, see Richard P. Nathan, Philip M. Dearborn, Clifford A. Goldman, and Associates, "Initial Effects of the Fiscal Year 1982 Reductions in Federal Domestic Spending," in Ellwood, *Reductions*.

appreciable fashion was the elimination of the public service employment program, which had different impacts in hard-pressed cities from those in the more prosperous ones.

In the more prosperous cities, the effects of eliminating PSE appear to have been negligible. Most of these cities had protected themselves against such an eventuality by subcontracting substantial numbers of PSE positions and concentrating these funds in services that could be easily terminated without establishing any claim on the city budget. As noted earlier, in 1978 Congress had imposed considerable restrictions on the types of persons who could be hired and on their maximum pay and tenure in PSE positions. Most of the prosperous places appear to have begun to reduce their involvement in the program at this point by reducing the number of PSE positions they retained in their own agencies and by moving former PSE workers they wished to retain onto the city payroll. Phoenix, for example, moved approximately 500 positions from PSE to city funding well before the program was eliminated, and Chicago shifted more than 350 slots.

Hard-pressed cities were hurt more by the PSE termination. Because of their fiscal position, these cities had been unable to reduce their participation in the program after the 1978 restrictions took effect. They were compelled either to seek waivers of program requirements or to continue participation under the more stringent regulations.

Boston, Rochester, and St. Louis were forced to reduce services after PSE ended. All three cities had come under increased fiscal pressure since 1978—Rochester as a result of a court-mandated rollback of property tax rates, and Boston and St. Louis as a result of major tax limitation measures. All were in the process of reducing city-funded work forces when PSE was terminated. As the St. Louis authors note:

[The elimination of PSE], involving a loss of $21 million to St. Louis, is a severe blow because of the city's heavy reliance on PSE workers to supplement its regular civil service complement, which itself has now been significantly reduced. . . . This reduction in federal aid comes at a particularly inopportune time because of the climate produced because of the tax resistance movement. . . . Confronted with a threatened initiative referendum to abolish the 10 percent utility tax, the Board of Aldermen in 1979 passed a law phasing out the levy on residential users by 1973. When fully in effect the repeal will reduce tax revenues by about $24 million a year.[5]

Detroit and Cleveland, by contrast, were able to avoid major

5. Henry J. Schmandt, George D. Wendel, and E. Allan Tomey, *Federal Aid to St. Louis* (Washington, D.C.: Brookings Institution, 1983), p. 66.

layoffs when PSE ended by securing large increases in local
income tax rates. While the Cleveland increase passed relatively
easily, the Detroit increase was the result of a long, complex, and
bitterly contested campaign. State legislative approval was
required to place the increase on the ballot. The legislature gave
its approval, but required the city to secure substantial wage concessions from city employees and to sell city bonds to eliminate a
$120 million deficit. The city was able to meet all conditions, but
only after a major lobbying effort, and is confronting another siz-
able deficit as a result of reductions in state aid and worsening
economic conditions.[6]

A second factor that may have lessened the impact of federal
cuts on the cities under consideration here has been the increased
flexibility in the use of Community Development Block Grant
funds made available by both Congressional and administration
action. The Department of Housing and Urban Development has
sharply curtailed federal review of CDBG applications, has re-
pealed the requirement that CDBG funds be "targeted" on low-
and moderate-income groups, and has permitted local governments
to use appreciable amounts of CDBG funds to support on-going
services. While the administration's proposal to eliminate gradually
restrictions on the use of CDBG funds seems unlikely to pass, the
extension of the program currently being debated by Congress
calls for increasing the share of funds that can be spent on services,
thus allowing harder pressed cities to use enhanced amounts of
CDBG funds to support basic services. While this increased
flexibility does not completely offset the loss of PSE funds, it may
limit the adverse effect of this loss on local services.[7]

The importance of this point should not be overstated. With
the exception of Boston, the hard-pressed cities rely more heavily
on cyclically sensitive revenue sources, such as city income and
sales taxes, than do most other cities. This reliance makes them
particularly vulnerable if the current recession continues. Further, Rochester and Boston have had to adjust to substantial losses
in property tax revenues over the last three years. The loss of PSE
funds has worsened these cities' fiscal burdens appreciably. If,
however, federal operating grants are approved at levels roughly

6. Thomas Anton, *Federal Aid to Detroit* (Washington, D.C.: Brookings Institution, 1983), chapter 7.
7. For a more detailed description and assessment of the changes in CDBG,
see Michael Rich, "Fiscal and Political Implications of the CDBG Experience in
10 Cities," paper presented at the Midwest Political Science Association Annual
Meeting, April, 1983.

equivalent to those proposed in the administration's fiscal 1984 budget, things will not get any worse as a result of further reductions in federal funds.

The impact of the Reagan budget cuts on this set of cities, in sum, has been considerably smaller than had been previously predicted, in part because programs that supply funds to city governments have not been reduced as substantially as those that provide support to other types of governments, but more importantly because of strategies adopted by many cities to insulate themselves from the adverse results of possible reductions in federal support. While harder pressed cities have had considerably more difficulty in adjusting to these reductions than cities with fewer financial problems, the impact of reduced federal support in these places has been less catastrophic than was anticipated.